Changes in Transportation

by Barbara Wood

PEARSON

Scott
Foresman

Editorial Offices: Glenview, Illinois • Parsippany, New Jersey • New York, New York
Sales Offices: Needham, Massachusetts • Duluth, Georgia • Glenview, Illinois
Coppell, Texas • Ontario, California • Mesa, Arizona

Jo wants to see a friend. Jo's friend lives nearby. Jo will ride a bike or travel by car.

Andy wants to see his friend too. Andy's friend lives far away. Andy will travel by airplane to see his friend.

Long ago, people did not have many choices about how to travel. They often had to walk wherever they wanted to go. They carried their things on their heads or strapped them to their backs.

People did not travel unless they had to. Traveling was hard, slow work. In some places this is still true.

As time went by, people tried to find easier ways to travel. They learned that animals could help with the work. Camels, donkeys, and horses could carry big loads on their backs. These animals could also carry people. They could even pull carts, wagons, or sleds.

People learned they could make things go too. They peddled bicycles, skated, and pulled carts.

To travel on rivers and lakes, people learned to build rafts and canoes. For traveling on the ocean, people made strong sailing ships. These ships used sails and wind to travel on the seas. People had learned that there were many ways to travel on the water.

Most travel was still not fast or easy. Few people traveled far from home. Soon one **invention** changed travel.

This invention was the **engine**. An engine is a machine that makes things move. Ships no longer needed sails. Instead they used steam engines to move. So did the first trains.

Gas engines were used in the first cars. The Wright brothers also used a gas engine when they invented the first airplane.

Travel became much faster. Trains carried huge loads. Miles of roads and railroads were built.

People used many new types of **vehicles** to travel!

Ford Model T Car

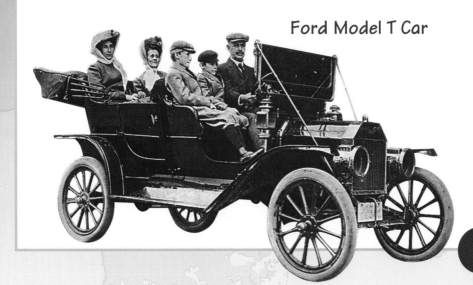

New vehicles are fast. They ride smoothly. Computers help make some of these vehicles work. Some new vehicles help to save gasoline.

Many vehicles can go over bumps and snow. Others can speed across water. Some vehicles can even travel back and forth to outer space!

The story of transportation is not over yet! People are hard at work to bring us new kinds of vehicles. Travel is going to keep changing. What do you think will be the next kind of vehicle?

Glossary

engine a machine that makes things move

invention something new

vehicle something that carries people or
things, such as a car

Write to It!

How do you travel from place to place? Tell two things you like about this kind of travel and two things you do not.

Write your answers on another sheet of paper.

Fun Facts

- Many of the first sailing ships had oarsmen. If there was no wind, they rowed the ship with oars.

- The first airplane could not fly high or fast. It could not even fly over a house.

- Many old trains burned coal to make them go.

Genre	Comprehension Skill	Text Features
Nonfiction	Predict	• Glossary • Illustrations • Captions

Scott Foresman Social Studies

PEARSON

Scott Foresman

scottforesman.com

ISBN 0-328-14806-7

90000

9 780328 148066

The Shape of Our Land

by Ann Rossi

The United States is a country that has many different areas and a variety of natural features, such as bodies of water. In this book you will learn about some of the natural features found in the regions of the United States.

Vocabulary

region

prairie

desert

landform

mountain

erosion

volcano

plain

wetland

waterway

glacier

ISBN: 0-328-14841-5

2 3 4 5 6 7 8 9 10 V0G1 14 13 12 11 10 09 08 07 06 05